ON THE JOURNEY OF A
HEALING HEART

Gentle Steps

ON THE JOURNEY OF A
HEALING HEART

LIVING JOYFULLY THROUGH ROCKY TIMES

Clara Penner

BALBOA
PRESS

A DIVISION OF HAY HOUSE

Balboa Press books may be ordered through booksellers or by contacting:

Balboa Press
A Division of Hay House
1663 Liberty Drive
Bloomington, IN 47403
www.balboapress.com
1-(877) 407-4847

ISBN: 978-1-4525-4123-5 (sc)
ISBN: 978-1-4525-4125-9 (hc)
ISBN: 978-1-4525-4124-2 (e)

Library of Congress Control Number: 2011918810

Printed in the United States of America

Balboa Press rev. date: 10/24/2011

This book is dedicated to my family. To my husband, Curtis, for reminding us to always have fun, especially during the tough times; to Braxton, for sharing his ability to overcome obstacles with an unbroken spirit; and to Blayne, who guided us to stop and enjoy the journey.

I am forever grateful you are in my life!

I love you all!

Contents

Mission

I wrote this book to provide guidance for you to find the best you, the happiest you, the peaceful you! We all have these parts within us, but daily life and difficult situations deprive us of the one true thing we seek: a happy life! This book will give you the tools and support to find those parts within you once again; to find your wholeness, and to start living life the way you truly deserve!

The chapter narratives relate my family's personal experience. Chapters 1 through 7 each conclude with a section called "Gentle Steps," which serves as a kind of workbook relevant to the topics explored in that chapter's narrative.

Please be aware that the techniques described in this book are self-help and self-healing techniques, and you are in control of their use. As such, you have sole responsibility when you use them. I do not recommend substituting these techniques for the professional services or advice of a doctor, psychologist, psychiatrist, or any healthcare or mental-healthcare provider or practitioner.

The Diagnosis

Undoubtedly, you have experienced moments that changed your life forever. Whether good or bad, standing in those moments can make you feel like your DNA is changing right then and there. In these moments you can feel your heart break, or you can feel so happy you want to jump up and shout. But no matter what, you know this moment is going to shape your future and become a part of who you are. We all have been there.

Let me introduce myself: My name is Clara. I am a proud mother of two amazing kids, Braxton and Blayne; I am the wife of an incredible husband, Curtis. Individually and together as a family, we have shown each other how to live our best lives. Throughout this book I will share our moments with you . . . .

Our son, Braxton, was diagnosed with severe hemophilia when he was two days old. In the moment when the doctor told us, I felt a rush of every feeling I could imagine: pain, sadness, loss, insecurity, fear, and guilt. All of those feelings fused, forming what I thought would be a permanent knot in my stomach. I kept feeling like I was going to cry. Each time I swallowed it felt like my throat was closing. Never in my life had I felt fear so deep, so painful, so unwavering as the unknown that I now faced. The thought of losing this brand-new miracle I had just received in my life terrified me, sending me on a roller coaster of emotions that were more intense than anything I'd ever experienced. I spent most of the next seven days in the hospital, crying; I stopped only when I held my son and could see his precious smile. I basked in these moments, where I felt joy overpower fear and pain, even if only for a brief moment. Even though my hospital room was crowded with people, I had never felt so scared and so alone.

Curtis and I met with the hematologist, who explained to us that severe hemophilia is a bleeding disorder in which the blood is unable to clot properly. We could expect that Braxton would experience internal bleeding into his joints, muscles and possibly his organs, and this could occur with something as simple as a minor injury—or, even worse, spontaneously. The hematologist further explained that scratches would not be the problem, as they were visible to the naked eye and could be properly monitored. Internal bleeding, however, would be a serious problem, as this is not visible and therefore hard to identify and extremely difficult to monitor. The hematologist continued to outline the symptoms that Braxton might experience during an internal bleed, as well as what the steps of treatment would be. He went on to tell us about how we could treat Braxton intravenously, using a safe product that would help his blood to clot. This hematologist was one of the nicest men I'd ever met. His voice was filled with compassion as he honestly described what the future would hold for a hemophiliac and his family. Even though we did not know it at the time, this doctor would save Braxton's life multiple times. My husband and I both left that meeting feeling devastated, helpless, terrified, extremely lost, and unsure of our future.

Curtis and I both were in our early twenties when Braxton was born, and so we still had a lot of growing up to do—something else we did not know at the time. Nevertheless, we would have to finish growing up quickly, as we now had this miracle who needed us even more than a "normal" baby would have. We did not say much to each other on our way back to the hospital room. There were no words either of us could use to make the other feel better; there was nothing that anyone else could do or say to make this any better, either. I just went back to the room, held Braxton, and cried. I cried for the loss of what I had imagined the birth should have been; I cried for the loss of Braxton's being able to do things with ease as he grew; I cried for the fear of never wanting him to feel pain; I cried for the things we would have to go through; I cried for losing what I considered to be our "normal" life. I felt so much guilt, and I wondered why this had happened to us. I had always thought this kind of thing only happened to other people. I came to understand that, at times, any of us can be the "other people."

In life-changing moments such as these—the ones that bring you to your knees—you have to make a choice. You can choose either to reach for love and let it help lift you, or to do nothing and stay down. So I made my choice: I reached for love.

When we got home, I settled into the routine of parenting. I never had a dream of a career, as my dream had always been to be a mom. To me, that was the best job I could have, and there was nothing in this world that I wanted more. Even though the fear had a tight grip on me, and that knot in my stomach was always as big as it could be, I had never been happier. Every day my son was the light that kept me going. His smile, his laugh, everything about him radiated hope. He was all I needed to keep moving forward. As Braxton cuddled against me, I could see that he was such a treasure. Everything he did just made me happy. It was like unwrapping a gift each time he woke up or went to sleep or cooed or smiled. In these moments I began a remarkable, intense, yet deeply rewarding journey. This journey turned my world and every aspect of my belief system upside down; it flipped it, stomped on it, crushed it, and then reinvented it.

At the time I could not see that, because of this journey, I would begin to realize the value and beauty of life. I had to choose how each step of this journey would shape my life. Would it break me, or would it help me grow? To be honest, it did both. Sometimes we have to break in order to grow. When we reach for love it always helps us put the broken pieces back together, and then, as we go on, that new whole is stronger than the old one was. I always consciously made the choice to see the positive. No matter how dark things seemed to get, I saw beauty unveiled to my husband and me in ways we could never have imagined! In the moments when I felt I was at my lowest I needed to stop ask myself, *What am I grateful for?*

GENTLE STEPS

I know that nearly everyone has heard of how therapeutic journaling is, and I am going to say it again.

1. Start to Journal

I started one a **journal** and divided it into **four sections:**

- **Section 1** is where I journal my own thoughts.
- **Section 2** is where I journal my thoughts for my son.
- **Section 3** is where I journal my thoughts for my daughter (you will meet her a bit later on in the book).
- **Section 4** is where I journal my thoughts for my husband.

I also started a **gratitude journal.** Every day, I write about one thing that I am thankful for. This ensures that I always feel grateful, and that alone has gotten me far!

Never underestimate the attitude of gratitude!

No one saw my journals; as a result, journaling allowed me to release and share my thoughts when I was unable to voice them. It still does.

I was frightened of the whole idea of journaling. I was taught to keep my feelings inside, so I never knew how to express my feeling. Bringing light to those feelings can be very frightening at first. However, whether or not you admit your feelings, they are there, and bottling them up can do a lot more damage than releasing them. When you are aware of your feelings you are able to validate them, which is incredibly freeing.

Below are some examples to help you start your own journal. Once you begin to journal, just continue to write whatever thoughts and feelings come to your mind. It doesn't have to be organized—or even make sense—just continue to write and release your emotions. Remember, this is your journal, and there is no right or wrong way to journal!

2. Examples of How to Start

- I am so frustrated that the doctor . . . *sometimes does not listen.*
- I am so frustrated that my friend . . . *does not understand what I am going through.*
- I feel like I missed out on . . . *moments being the way I thought they would be.*
- These are the words that describe my life . . . *remarkable and blessed or chaotic and exhausting*
- I am so grateful for . . . *getting a peaceful shower today so I had a couple minutes to myself.*
- I love it when . . . *I get a surprise.*
- I am so grateful that my husband . . . *had the coffee ready for me when I got up.*
- I am so grateful that my child . . . *gave me a hug this morning. That set me up for a great day!*

Now write some of your own:

3. Have a Positive Conclusion

Always end your journaling on a positive note; conclude with your grateful thoughts, so you are in the attitude of gratitude. (It's up to you if you want to start a separate gratitude journal as well.) Make sure you keep it simple. Don't overthink it—you don't want journaling to become another "job" or item on your to-do list. Journaling should be something that helps you, and also that you have fun with. Make it your own process; there is no right or wrong method. Every moment, no matter how big or small, is a piece of your life's puzzle, so enjoy the journey of your life!

The Trials

As Braxton grew up, my family and I had the most precious memories—and we faced some of the biggest tests. We have seen the best and the worst in people. I could not possibly have prepared myself for the road ahead, but I had to find a way to travel it. As I went through muddy waters I found my personal power. When I started this journey, I would have described myself as very insecure and unsure of myself. I did not know how to stand up for myself, and I often let others walk all over me. Through these challenges with my son, I was determined to become the person I needed to be—the person I had to be—so that he would have the care he needed and deserved.

Journaling helped me realize that a lot of the frustration I felt came from other people's beliefs and fear-based misconceptions about hemophilia. People seemed so concerned with Braxton's restrictions that they overlooked all the things he *could* do. It felt as though the world sought to limit Braxton. Many times people would say things like "sorry about Braxton." I, too, was sorry about the things my son had to suffer through, but hemophilia was a part of him. To me, love means unconditional acceptance. That meant accepting every part of Braxton so that he could accept every part of himself. I decided it was time to reevaluate some of my own beliefs. I am so thankful I did this, because I set myself up for success without even knowing it. Often, and usually unconsciously, we allow others' fears and beliefs to limit us.

My family and I were about to start our journey down an uncharted road, but we had faith. Plus, we knew that we would progress along our path by designing our own set of beliefs along the way. This kind of journey is not always easy, but it is always worth it—and in our case there simply was no other way to go.

Curtis and I lived three hours away from the hematologist and the hospital equipped to handle Braxton's condition. As positive as our experience with the hematologist had been—even though he had to give us awful news—that's how negative our experience with the pediatrician in our area was. It was a disaster from the day we met this doctor, and it just kept getting worse. His ego outweighed his desire to properly treat our son with the care he needed. I tried to meet with others doctors in the city, but each one turned us away, refusing to take Braxton as a patient. I felt so lost; I could not understand how medical professionals could refuse treatment to an infant—or anyone else, for that matter.

The hematologist had warned Curtis and me that Braxton would begin having problems with bleeding, this happened the first time he rolled over; his hand would get stuck under his body, and as he pulled it out, the friction would cause an internal bleed in his hands and fingers. The area of the internal bleed swelled until Braxton could no longer move his fingers apart or in any direction; it looked like a big marshmallow. I rushed him into the pediatrician's office for treatment, but the doctor responded by saying he could see no problem. He turned around and just left the room. I was so stunned, I couldn't even react.

After collecting myself, I called Braxton's hematologist to tell him of the situation, and he was as shocked as I was. He told me that I would have to drive the three hours to the hospital where he worked in order for Braxton to receive the treatment he needed. The driving was not the problem—I would undertake a drive of any duration to help my children—it was the hours of pain that my son would have endure while he waited for proper treatment that bothered me. Nevertheless, this would happen over and over again with each of Braxton's bleeds. The first step he took resulted in a hip bleed. While learning to walk he experienced many tumbles, just as all kids do; however, with Braxton, this constant falling caused his body to bruise and bleed internally. Time after time, Braxton and I would have to make that three-hour drive so that he could receive treatment.

Even though it seemed that our options were running out, I refused to give up. I was not willing to stop until I found good care for Braxton.

At this point I began to search for things that would empower our situation—that would empower my family—and me. I wrote a letter to the Minister of Health explaining the situation, asking only for the care for my son needed and deserved. I did receive a personal call from her, and she was willing to help me find a doctor for my son. That proved a harder task than even she had thought. Three months later, however, she did find one doctor who was willing to take Braxton as a patient. It was not the ideal situation, as this doctor was often unavailable. Although this left us still searching for medical care during the times when Braxton's doctor was unavailable, Curtis and I found a glimmer of hope.

Curtis had grown up in a small town, a community of about one thousand people, which was about a half hour away from the city where we lived. There we found a doctor who was willing to provide any care that he could. Words are inadequate to express how much we appreciated this doctor and the medical staff there. Unfortunately, this small-town hospital could only handle administering the medication. The facility was unable to stabilize and transport Braxton if he needed to go to a bigger hospital in the event of a life-threatening bleed. Even though they did all they could, we still needed to find a place where Braxton would receive more comprehensive care.

Whenever we got to the small-town hospital, the doctor would always be there waiting, and he was so very kind. There is one time in particular that I remember. I brought Braxton to receive treatment for a bleed. Because he was so small—still a baby—it could sometimes be hard for the doctors to get the IV line into one of his veins. The bigger hospital in the city had a rule that each person had three tries to get a vein, and then someone else would try. After three tries, frustration would take over, decreasing the chance of getting the IV into the vein. As we now had one doctor and no other options, that rule could not apply. This doctor had a great reputation for being able to access even the smallest of veins; therefore, I knew Braxton was in very capable hands. Unfortunately, this time things did not go smoothly: twenty tries and misses on my nine-month-old son. We all were frustrated with missing the vein, so we took a little break. Braxton and I walked around a bit, and then we headed back into the hospital room. On the twenty-first time the doctor got the IV in, and Braxton got the medication he needed to start healing. Even though we had to do it all over again the next day, I was thankful Braxton had received the treatment he needed.

One thing that was always important to me was to be very honest with Braxton. If it was going to hurt, I would tell him, "Yes, it may hurt, but you have to trust Mom." Building trust with anyone is a process. We were in this for the long haul, and I needed him to trust me unconditionally. At times the medical professionals would be a little frustrated with this honesty, but I stuck with what I felt was right in my heart.

We were often judged by people because Braxton would get huge bruises on his body from the falls of learning to crawl and walk. When we were at home I would always make him wear knee pads, elbow pads, and a helmet. We removed from our house any furniture that had hard edges; we bought padded furniture; we installed very thick plush carpet. Luckily, we had a small house, so we could easily keep Braxton in the living room without feeling that we were confining him. This space was soft because of the changes we'd made, and it protected him when he started to learn to crawl and walk. These times were bittersweet for my husband and me. As Braxton took the natural steps of growing, we were so proud—and yet so fearful. I had such a roller-coaster of emotions with every new step. My heart would shine with pride for him one moment, and then break the next when he would endure a painful fall. I always missed that we couldn't enjoy these moments without the pain.

To get out of the house, we thought swimming would be a fun and safe way for Braxton to be active. So off I went to sign up for the Mommy and Me swimming. The first day, not one parent or instructor would come near us, leaving us excluded from the swim games and lessons. Why? Because Braxton had about eight baseball-size bruises. I can't say what they thought had happened to him, but I was shocked at their treatment of my son. As a mom, of course the judgments hurt, but not as much as the alienation of my child. I continued to go for three more lessons, but after that I stopped going. Every time we came home I would cry; the whole experience left my heart heavy and sad.

It was at this time that I got involved with the hemophilia organization, hoping to improve my search for available treatment options for Braxton. In effort to be proactive, I became a board member and eventually the President of Hemophilia Saskatchewan, and also a board member of the Canadian Hemophilia Society.

As I traveled around Canada I became immersed in finding solutions that helped my son and other families. Meeting others who understood these challenges was a gift. Many people we met helped shape my future; they also helped my family heal. As helpful as these organizations were to us personally, we were still not getting the care Braxton needed from the local doctors.

Seven days before Braxton's first birthday, I woke to a painful quiet cry. I immediately ran from my bed to Braxton's room across the hall. Braxton was having a seizure, and he had thrown up all over his crib. His usually bright blue eyes were a cloudy gray. When I picked him up he was limp. I screamed, and my husband was at my side before I could even call his name. He took Braxton, grabbed the keys to the car, and flew out of the house. I stood by the crib, paralyzed with fear. It seemed like forever before I was able to move.

Finally I ran to the phone and called my dad; I was crying so hard that I could not even breathe. All my dad said was, "Who is this?" I am the youngest of six children, so he needed to know who he was rescuing! "Clara" was all I could manage, but it was all my dad needed to hear. It seemed as if my dad had teleported to my house. I heard my doorbell ring and, still in my pj's, ran back to the car with my dad. My dad still had no idea what had happened, and I was still crying too hard to be able speak. When we got to the hospital, the nurse led me right to my son; no words were spoken. There were no words that could comfort me—all I wanted was to hold my son and never let him go! The hospital staff was in a flurry. My husband disagreed with the treatment, so he called the specialists in an effort to get the proper treatment. The panic and fear were so thick you could cut them with a knife. It was so surreal, I felt as if I were watching a movie.

But then something incredible happened. As I looked into Braxton's gray and lifeless eyes I seemed to connect with his soul. This is the most magical moment I have ever experienced. The world seemed to stop. For a moment the fear dissipated, and I felt a glimmer of hope. Desperate, I asked my son to find his way back to me—and to never give up. I promised him that I would not give up, either; I promised him that, together, we could overcome anything. All too soon reality snapped me back into the flurry of panic, but I retained the feeling of that moment and the sense of hope. Moments later the air ambulance team arrived. Letting go of my son's small hand, I let the team take over. Watching the elevator doors close, my hope rested in the fact Braxton had heard my promise.

We were unable to go in the air ambulance because it was full of medical staff. Curtis and I drove the three hours to University Hospital, where we immediately went to look for our son. He was in the pediatric intensive care (PIC) unit. The doctors had found that Braxton had a spontaneous brain hemorrhage. When I looked at Braxton now, I could see the natural blue of his eyes emerging from the dull gray. I knew he had heard my promise. I thought to myself, *If he can do this he can do anything.* As for me, I had made the promise, and I intended to keep it. I was not going to let my son down—not now, not ever. He came through for me; now it was my turn to come through for him.

The recovery took almost a year. Braxton underwent numerous tests—CAT scans, MRIs, blood tests, and so forth—to make sure he was healing properly. He ate very little, and he threw up a lot. He had a hard time walking, and I can't even begin to describe how bad the headaches were. We spent all day cuddling, giving his little body time to heal. My husband and I played a record amount of cribbage in Braxton's hospital room. Playing cards gave us something else to focus on, and it helped us keep our spirits up. Such long amounts of time in the hospital can really get a person feeling down. We would not leave Braxton alone; one of us was always with him. You start to miss the fresh air and the things you take for granted when at home. The sound of constantly beeping monitors and people going in and out of the room became normal. The little cots that we slept on did not seem so bad; I was able to hold Braxton's hand, which let me know that he was okay, and that made the world perfect. My husband loved to get Braxton out of his room. He would grab a little wagon, make a bed for him, and off we would go making circles around the hospital. It felt good to move around, and we found a lot of interesting things and met interesting people on our walks.

While Braxton was in the hospital, they inadvertently had been overdosing him on antiseizure meds, which went on for a week without anyone noticing. After many tests to make sure that he did not suffer any damage from the overdose, he seemed to be okay. This experience made us realize that all healthcare professionals are human and can make mistakes. As a result of this, we understood how important it was for us to be proactive in regard to our son's healthcare and the health and care of our whole family at all times.

Curtis and I decided that we both needed to train to learn home care. This would be the best option, because we would be able to give Braxton all the treatments ourselves, eliminating some of the time spent waiting in the hospital. Even when it would be necessary to drive Braxton the three hours to the hematologist, home care would allow us to give him preliminary treatment first. Braxton had an operation to insert a Port-A-Cath, which we would use to administer his treatments as a way to help save his veins. With home care, Curtis and I would be able to continue the treatments Braxton received in the hospital. This allowed us to get out of the hospital two months after the team had airlifted Braxton there. Once home, we would need to continue Braxton's IV treatments four times a day. These treatments would help his blood clot, and we would be able to gradually cut down the number of treatments until, eventually, he would only need a prophylactic treatment once a day, three times a week. We also had to continue the antiseizure meds for three months at home.

Braxton would have to go back for many more tests all throughout the following year. He had problems with speech, so he started to work with a speech therapist, which would continue for another four years. After that he had no further problems with speech. It was a long recovery, but each day, I was grateful for how much he improved. Every baby step he took was a gift. His hematologists monitored him through his growing years to see what damage, if any, he sustained as a result of the brain hemorrhage. (Years later he still finds that he does have to be careful about shaking of his head too much, which can give him headaches; but for the most part he came through it just fine.)

Braxton seemed to be doing very well during the six months after the brain hemorrhage; that is, until Thanksgiving weekend of 1999. I was visiting my parents, and Braxton had fallen asleep, so I decided to have my parents watch him while I went home to do some cleaning and laundry. I had just started when my mom called me to let me know that something was wrong with Braxton: his bowel movements were huge amounts of pure blood. I rushed back to their house and took Braxton to the ER doctor.

The ER doctor confirmed that Braxton had a gastrointestinal bleed. This meant he was bleeding into his stomach. Shockingly enough, the doctor sent us home—no treatments, no ambulance, nothing—he said to just go home and wait for it to stop. Somehow he must have missed the memo that my son's blood was unable to clot. Thankfully, because we'd started home care, we knew what to do. I went home, and Curtis and I treated Braxton. We called the hematologist to let him know what was happening. He told us we needed to get Braxton to University Hospital immediately. In an instant we were on the highway, headed for the hospital three hours away. Curtis drove as fast as he could, but the traffic was bad because it was a holiday weekend. Halfway there, Braxton passed out from blood loss. I called the hospital to let them know, and the hematologist immediately sent an ambulance to take Braxton the rest of the way, as well as a police escort to get Curtis and me there quickly and safely. Unfortunately, we missed them both. When we arrived at the hospital the staff was waiting at the doors for Braxton, taking him in for immediate treatment. Braxton needed a blood transfusion, a dozen different tests, and many treatments. Once again he became our miracle. After six weeks we were able to go home.

After that Braxton had two more surgeries to insert Port-A-Cath devices, plus a few muscle and joint bleeds. For the most part, as he grew up, it got a little easier; he could tell us where it hurt and how much, so it was less of a guessing game. When he was nine years old, he took over my job and started self-care at home, which meant that he began giving himself his own IV treatments. He loved the independence it gave him, and he was great at it. Over the four years that Braxton has been giving himself his own meds, he has only missed his vein about six times. He even gave himself meds when he had a broken arm and was in a cast for four months; he did not miss even once! Curtis and I never doubted Braxton's ability, and so he never doubted himself, either. He just did it. I was amazed, but after all the experiences that we had with children with illness, we understood how amazing these special children were, and we never really doubted anything. It seemed that children with healthcare challenges have an innately unbreakable spirit that is simply amazing. I believe that once you see past all the painful experiences these kids face, you will see the amazing gift and light they are in the world.

GENTLE STEPS

1. Evaluate Your Belief System

Ask yourself, *What is my belief system?*

Your belief system is made from beliefs you have been taught about situations in life—about money, work, or anything. Often we adapt these beliefs to our lives, never challenging them to see if they still serve us in the present moment. As we change and grow, so do our needs—and so can our beliefs. We must have an open awareness of why we do what we do, as this is the only honest way to see if it still works for us. Being aware of your belief system—and being open to letting go of those beliefs that no longer serve you—will help you grow in all areas of your life. Your belief system can limit you, unconsciously, from achieving your goals. In answering the next questions be very honest and take your time.

What are the limitations that keep you from achieving your goals?

What are your beliefs around those limitations?

Do you feel that your beliefs still serve you, or are you open to challenging them?

What new beliefs would work to replace limitations in your situation?

What are the pros and cons of the new belief(s)?

What limitations do you put on your loved ones?

What are your beliefs around those limitations?

Do you feel that your beliefs still serve you, or are you open to challenging them?

What new beliefs would work to replace the limitations in your situation?

What are the pros and cons of the new beliefs?

2. Never Underestimate the Value of You!

This section is dedicated to giving you the credit you deserve. Often we do not give ourselves credit for our accomplishments, big or small, and this kind of credit is very important. As you accomplish things in your life, use them as stepping-stones to build you up. This may be hard, but it is so important; think back on all the things that you're proud of, and write them down. Acknowledge *you*.

List the top five accomplishments of each one of your family members, big and small, that make you proud. You could have each one of your family members do this, and then share with each other. This would help everyone establish an attitude of gratitude!

1.

2.

3.

4.

5.

3. Contact Support

Support groups can be found through the hospital, Internet, or phone book.

It can be so helpful to have someone to talk to. Perhaps you have a good friend or family member to share with. Often it can also be helpful to have others who have been in the same situation. There are many ways you can find support, depending on what you are going through. Finding others who know how you feel can make you feel less isolated; they also can guide you, based on their own experience.

living life

It can be difficult to live life in the face of constant trials. Working through the emotional roller coaster of the whole family can leave you feeling drained and exhausted. Fears of what could happen can also place many limitations on living life to the fullest. At least this was my experience. I felt I had the whole world on my shoulders, and I always felt fearful about what might happen. Never knowing what challenges lay ahead caused me to feel lost in a sea of the unknown. Braxton loved living life, and I never wanted my fear to hold him back. I did a lot of inner work to deal with my emotions; at first, I felt guilty for how I felt.

One of my long-held beliefs had been that, in order to be a good mom, you must sacrifice; the more that you sacrificed, the better a person you would become. Therefore, my belief about myself became that I had to sacrifice in order be a good mom and a good person. Through our trials I found that the opposite was true: being a player in my life (by which I mean living it to the fullest) was of vital importance—far more so than sacrificing—and it would set my family on a better path. The more balanced I became, the more balanced my family became. It truly was one of the most amazing transformations I have ever seen. Everything is about balance.

My family has found the most beautiful people, and we have had some of the most amazing experiences during our most rocky times. The one thing that we always respected was everyone's personal story, because each one helped us see the amazing strength, courage, and passion of the human spirit. Watching others live life while going through challenges helped us do the same. Braxton was the happiest kid I had ever seen; nothing really angered or upset him. The same was true for many of the children we met on our journey. These children handled unimaginable hurdles in life with more grace and faith than one could imagine. If you ever need to see the pure loving spirit, it is apparent in the last place you would ever imagine: the children's ward of a hospital. This is where you can see children teaching others to be the true light and love that we all seek!

Curtis, Braxton, and I met some amazing children during our times in the hospital—children and people who would change our lives for the better. I would like to share some of those stories with you.

When Braxton was a baby, we had gone to an appointment at the same time as the patients from a children's cancer clinic. As I sat there afraid, this little girl came up to chat with me. She asked me all about my baby, and I felt so at peace in her presence. It was her pure love for life that touched me so deeply. This child was not afraid of the future or the next treatment; she just was living in the moment. I could not believe the peace that I saw in her.

Before Braxton underwent surgery in insert the Port-A-Cath, we had met with a little boy who also had a port, so that we could ask him and his mom some questions. They had been in the hospital for months, and the little boy chatted about how he had been in the hospital through Christmas—at that point, it was March—but he thought that he might get out around Easter for a bit. His mom was just as hopeful and optimistic. They were kind and giving with their time and energy, the most precious gifts of all. We were so grateful, and we wanted to pay it forward.

I can't even tell you how many children Curtis would just start up conversations with, or how many games he played or books he read to kids. But the one he will never forget was a boy named Phil, who had been hit by a car, had lots of broken bones, and could not leave his bed at all. I can't remember how their friendship started, but I do remember that Braxton was in the hospital for about six weeks, and during that whole time Curtis was the only visitor that Phil had. When Braxton and I were napping, Curtis would read books to Phil, or just sit in his room and chat. Often Phil would ask the nurses to come get Curtis. To this day, if you ask Curtis which child was the most memorable, he will always answer, "Phil."

There was Chase, another boy who was such an amusing kid. He had been transported by air ambulance before Braxton was admitted.

This boy's love for life lit up the room. He had come to the hospital with nothing—no clothes, not even a toothbrush. Braxton had given him a hockey card, and this boy treated it like it was a precious heirloom. After hearing the many stories of that this boy had shared with us, Braxton could see he lived quite differently from us. We all listened to his stories—many were funny, and some were sad—but we all just enjoyed the conversations. He told us about playing hockey with his friends at the police station. Braxton was in shock, as he was used to playing hockey on the street. Even with the different life experiences, it seemed as though we all connected through the common experience of healing.

There was also the other Braxton, who had been named after my Braxton, which was the most touching story to me. When my Braxton was in the hospital for his gastrointestinal bleed, another boy named Braxton was admitted in the bed right across from him. For safety reasons we changed rooms, as we did not want either child to end up with the wrong meds or the wrong operation. As we were leaving the room, the other Braxton's mom asked me if my son had been in the pediatric intensive care (PIC) unit about six months before. I said that he had been there at that time, receiving treatment for a brain hemorrhage. The mom told me that her daughter was in the room next to my son's, but she had not made it out—it seemed as though she might not ever be able to leave the PIC unit. When my Braxton was transferred the girl's mom asked the nurse what his name was. All the nurse was at liberty to tell her was that his first name was Braxton. The woman was pregnant at the time, and my Braxton had given her hope that her child could one day leave the PIC unit, just as he had done. Because of the hope that Braxton gave her, she named her son after him.

I could go on for chapters and chapters just relating stories about the amazing people we have met—but that would be a whole book of its own. I just know that I can tell you, without a doubt, there are more inspiring people in the world than negative ones . . . you just have to open your eyes, and your heart, to see them.

When I am told about all the darkness in the world, I believe it's only how you see it. We used as examples the people and children we met, in addition to watching our own children (Braxton has a younger sister, Blayne, whom you will soon meet), and let them be the light we needed to help us live our own lives. Even though we do take extra safety precautions with Braxton, we allow him to participate in almost all activities. Curtis and I love the time we get to spend just hanging out with the kids. My entire family loves water sports, and Braxton is no exception—he tubes and wakeboards along with the rest of us. He plays on his junior-high basketball team, and is planning on becoming more competitive in basketball. One day he hopes to get a basketball scholarship for college. Braxton also loves ball hockey; and of all the positions to play, he is the goalie. And he loves it! It has taken a lot of working through my fears to allow him to live his dreams. But I am so glad I did, because watching him live his life to the fullest is a major gift to me. He has taught me not just to survive life, but to live it, love it, and be a part of it. Living life to the fullest is not just for a few, it is for everyone, but doing so is a choice we have to make.

As Braxton grew he would look at obstacles, no matter how big they might be, knowing that we could—and would—find our way through. If I could describe our life as a picture or metaphor, it would be a mountain that we would look up at, saying, "Look at that mountain, Braxton, we have to turn around." To which Braxton would say, "That mountain? No biggie! Let's climb it—I bet the other side is great!" And then he would take my hand, and off he would go. Braxton's view of the world leaves the rest of us sitting in amazement. I got so accustomed to using the "Braxton method"—that obstacles were no problem—I just knew we would get through the next obstacle whenever it came along. And, again and again, we did exactly that. It seemed that, together, we could conquer anything.

But then my daughter came along, and she had a whole new lesson to teach me. Blayne would race with us through the obstacle, but she also would want to stop and check out things along the way. I was so focused that I felt as though we could not stop. She kept insisting to literally smell the roses along the way. Eventually, we did find enjoyment in stopping and enjoying the journey. Now we were able to see the world along the way. I know each member of my family holds a piece of the puzzle; when we put it all together, it creates a beautiful picture.

My husband, like many people, is a kid at heart. He works hard and plays hard. It never mattered how sad the moment was, Curtis can break it up and make it fun. My favorite story was when Braxton was in the hospital with a brain hemorrhage, and my parents and one of my sisters had driven up to visit. Just as they parked, Curtis was leaving to get us some lunch. He had seen my parents, but my parents had not seen him, so he hid, snuck up on my mom, grabbed her purse, and ran away. My mom started yelling; my dad and my sister had not even gotten out of the car, and yet all they could see was Curtis running with the purse. When he turned back they all laughed. Who would have guessed that he even would have been in a joking mood, given all that was going on?

But my husband's whole theory is that if you have fun, it will all seem better. Turns out, he was on to something. It was harder for me than it was for him—to make everything fun, I mean—but I kept trying, and it did become easier for me, eventually. Even though I felt broken at the start of this journey, I began to feel that I was making myself whole again.

GENTLE STEPS

In order to be fulfilled you need to grow and contribute!

1. Design Your Ideal Day

From the moment you wake up until you go to bed, plan your ideal day:

These are the things that you can try to start putting into your day until this becomes a natural part of how you live every day. If you want to live more joyfully, you have to start adding things to your everyday routine that make you more joyful. Even the small things make a big difference. Now I know you may already be starting a list of reasons why you cannot do this, so here is step 2.

2. See Limits as Opportunities!

Turn all your "I can't _____" statements into "I am open to _____" statements:

As long as you make yourself believe that you can't, you will never be open to change. Once you are open to change, you will be amazed at what can happen. By being open to seeing in other ways, you will be able to see a bigger view, and realize that you have more options. By eliminating the word *can't* from your vocabulary, the excuses go away, and you realize all that is left is opportunity!

3. Control Your Fears and Design Your Dreams!

If you feel fear about something, somewhere in your life you are not prepared for this next step. Find the area where you need to strengthen, and then the fear will no longer exist.

Here is an example. If you are scared of water, you can do one of two things: never go near water again, or realize that this is an area that needs to be strengthened. If you choose the latter you could go get proper swimming lessons, which would strengthen the area where you feel fear. As you prepare yourself your fear will lessen, and you will eventually be able to swim. Also realize that fear is a warning and a gift: it lets you know that you have a weak area, and you need to prepare to handle the situation. By being aware of the fears and areas that need to be strengthened, you will be able to control the fear and design your dreams!

What are your fears?

Which areas does your fear make you aware that you need to strengthen?

What action steps can you take to strengthen those areas?

4

Letting Go

How do we let go? This is the million-dollar question. Here is one question that I always ask myself honestly: *Where I can improve in order to help my kids and myself?* After I answer that question, I ask myself some others: *How well have I prepared my kids and myself for this next step? What can I do to prepare them and myself in a healthy and nonintrusive manner? What actions do I need to take in order to help them and myself?*

One of the biggest and hardest lessons I learned was this: the best way to teach my kids was to be a good role model for them. No matter the situation, I always do this without fail.

I came to see that when I was not consistent, my kids were not sure what to do or how to react. I would say one thing and then do the opposite. Learning how to parent can be a challenge, and navigating through the maze of what was the right thing and what was the wrong thing proved exhausting. However, the kids always acted based on what they had seen more than on what I told them. My biggest lesson toward achieving my own growth was that I needed to become the person I wanted them to be. I had to learn how not to underestimate the power of me. It occurred to me that if I told my children, "Go climb that mountain," but they observed me sitting at the bottom saying, "Well, I can't, but you can," they would most likely sit there with me, because I was not showing them *how* to climb that mountain. I was not being a good role model. And as a result they each would likely think: *If it's so easy, why is Mom—who I love, trust, and look up to—unable to climb it? And if she can't how the heck can I do it? How come she says I can, if she can't?*

This stopped me in my tracks. I could not use the excuse that success is only for the chosen few, because I already had come to believe that we all have the same opportunities. I'd already learned that if I was not sure how to accomplish what I needed to, I could ask someone who knew how to help or guide me. Asking for help or guidance when needed is part of being a positive role model; knowing you need assistance is not the same as convincing yourself that you "can't"! This was what I needed to show my kids.

And so that's what I did. By showing my kids that "I could do it," they felt empowered too. I could only give what I honestly felt. Because they felt safe trusting me, they came to feel safe trusting themselves. I had discovered that everyone is born with their own internal guidance system—many call this *intuition*—I taught my kids to listen to their own guidance system, and to trust it. Not trusting myself had limited me significantly throughout my life up to that point, and so it was important to me that I taught my children how to listen to and trust themselves. When we trust our inner guidance we are being true to who we are, and this nurtures our souls. This was what I wanted my kids to do, but they wouldn't know how unless I showed them how; again, the only way I could do that was to be a good role model!

Up to that point I'd always struggled with listening to and trusting that inner guidance. I would feel my body—or the deepest part of me—trying to guide me in a certain direction, but then someone else (society or whoever it might have been that I thought knew better than I did) would tell me it was wrong. Looking back, I could have saved myself a lot of pain if I would have listened to and trusted what I truly felt. When I started to listen to my feelings and my body, I could finally breathe. At times I had to remind myself that we each have our own set of gifts and talents, and by letting my kids' gifts and talents shine through, they would be able to live lives of self-fulfillment. My way may not be the right way for either or both of them; staying open to their showing me their light was the best way to guide everyone.

I stopped living in fear, and I started to feel excited about being a part of this blossoming life. I became a player in my life. I remembered my dreams of the future, before any diagnosis had intruded, and it was simply this: I wanted to be a great mom, and I wanted whatever children I might have to be happy and enjoy life to the fullest! Even though the path was not what I expected it would be, I realized that I could still live those same dreams; I just needed to be open to how those dreams manifested. I needed to accept a different picture, so to speak. I stopped living in fear, but sometimes I still felt fear, just as we all do. When I felt that fear start to overwhelm me, I found it helpful to focus on something bigger that the fear. And so I would recall my forgotten or surrendered dreams, seeking to find ways to make them reality.

Each time I followed my heart, I felt freer and more alive. Many people along the way tried to guide me to stop, but I could not—and I didn't want to! I wanted my light to shine so that I could be the change I wanted to see. I knew that the people who tried to stop me meant well; they sought to save me from failure, but that was really their own fear of failing, not mine. To me, failing meant giving up on myself and those I loved. The more I followed my passion, the easier it was to create the life I wanted. I focused on my dreams with absolute faith and purpose; in doing so, I learned where I needed to grow. Best of all, I was able to do this in spite of fear!

GENTLE STEPS

1. Learning to Let Go

Below are the questions I described asking myself at the beginning of this chapter. Now it's your turn to ask and answer them, in terms of your and your family's experiences.

Where can I improve in order to help my kids and myself?

How well have I prepared them and myself for this next step?

What can I do to prepare them and myself in a healthy and nonintrusive manner?

What actions do I need to take in order to help them and myself?

2. Live the Life You Choose!

Now you need to determine whether the way you are living your life is the way that you *choose* to live your life.

Ask yourself, "Why am I doing what I am doing in my life?"

Now ask yourself, "Does what I do align me with my highest values and fondest dreams?"

If your fearful motivations drive your answers to the above, you can do one of two things: change *what* you are doing with your life, or change *why* you are doing it.

3. The "Inspired Why"

The truth is, you may not be able to change the *what,* but you probably can change the *why*—or at least your approach to it. If changing the *what* is not an option, create an **"inspired why"**! That is, redefine the *why* of where you are now until you can change the situation (i.e., the *what*). This *why* will help you live life as you choose; it will help you create a life filled with joy. That's what an **inspired why** is! If you understand and are deeply inspired by this *why,* eventually, you will begin to connect with others whom your *why* will also inspire; they will want to support and encourage you, and that will help you carry your *why*. Your *why* should be powered by your heart, not your head. Become crystal clear about your *why;* love it and live it!

Create *your* "inspired why":

4. Live Life with Purpose!

This goes back to what I said earlier about finding something bigger than the hurt and the fear, as this will help you let go of that fear and pain. First, make a **"purpose statement."** The real purpose of life is life itself! You need to live this life, enjoy this life, and embrace this life by living in the uniqueness of you! Here is a purpose statement that might help you create your own:

> *The purpose of my life is to be fully <u>alive</u> and <u>vibrant</u>, to enjoy this life living in the uniqueness of me, to adore and appreciate my loved ones, to guide others to feel fully alive, and to strengthen and share my gifts so that I might inspire others to strengthen and share their own gifts.*

Create *your* purpose statement, underlining the words that are most important to you, as in the example above:

Now, using the words that are most meaningful to you (i.e., the ones you underlined), answer the questions that follow. [Below, I have used the words that I underlined as examples; please use your own words in order to derive the most meaning from this exercise.]

What make you feel more alive and vibrant?

Whatever that is, do more of it!

What are you gifts?

Whatever they are, share them more often!

The above exercises have helped you make a "map" of what makes you feel positive and happy. Incorporating more of those things in your life will allow you to experience more positive emotion!

5

Our Journey
as Parents

Growing up, I was not confident; I always felt fearful. Speaking my mind was extremely difficult. I never imagined that I could become the person I am today! I always dreamed of being the person I have become: confident, creative, and comfortable being myself. I wanted to enjoy being me just as I was, but I did not know how I could get to that place. Now I do enjoy being me just as I am, but only because I have learned how to be a player in my own life. Looking back, I realize that life's journey is really just growing and blossoming into who we are meant to be, but who that is always changes, because life always changes. As long as you continue to grow and contribute—as long as you are a player in your own life—you can achieve any goal! This is what I did, and you can do it too.

Curtis and I were young when we married, as I mentioned. Even though we thought we were "all grown up," we had a lot more growing up to do. Facing and overcoming Braxton's trials was part of that, but our relationship had other challenges, just as every relationship does. Our marriage seemed filled with ever-present difficult lessons. We both were, and are, very loving people. We loved each other, and we still do; but our relationship often seemed turbulent, even before we became parents.

Braxton was a wonderful surprise, but we had no idea how much a baby would change our world. I don't think anyone can imagine how much becoming a parent will change his or her life—until it happens. That is true for all parents, not just those who have specific challenges to face, as we did with Braxton.

We struggled financially, so once we found out that we were expecting a baby, we knew we needed to make some changes in our work situation to accommodate the upcoming new expenses. This became essential after Braxton was born, as we would have even more medical expenses because of his health challenges. Curtis and I agreed that I would not return to my job; instead, I would stay home with Braxton. As a result, Curtis resigned from his job in the automotive industry and went to work in the oil patch, where he could earn a higher salary. This job would allow him to earn enough to replace both our former salaries, and also cover the extra expenses. However, this came at a cost to our family, as the work in the oil patch entails long hours many days in a row. This did not leave much time for family or recreation, only work. Curtis had to quit playing senior hockey, which was his passion, because his new job did not accommodate for any outside recreation activity. His job became his life. When he did get time off, he wanted to relax and go out with his friends. As for me, I felt very isolated and alone. My only focus was taking care of Braxton. Our resentment toward each other grew, and we began casting blame on each other for anything and everything. As individuals we were so positive and loving; as parents we were positive and loving; but, together in our marriage, we were not. Life as a couple became increasingly difficult, and we left a trail of blame and hurt.

After having Braxton, it seemed like I had to deal with one challenge after another, with no end in sight. I felt like I was always chasing something, trying in vain to stop the disorder. It kept me constantly busy; I became immersed in hemophilia. In truth, it became my whole life, consuming me and causing me to miss out on a lot.

When I gave birth to our second child, Blayne, she was a blessing that came just in time. She showed me that I needed to stop and enjoy life; Blayne taught me about balance. Blayne and Braxton are as different as night and day, each has been the divine blessing I needed, exactly when I needed it. Blayne is a sweet, kind, and caring little lady, but she is strong at heart. She has an innate knowing about her that just makes you just stop. While others might label this as "stubborn" or "difficult," I would describe it as a "knowing inner guidance"—one that I encourage her to heed and trust, as I've already explained.

When Blayne was two years old I became very ill. I was on a plane headed to Montreal for a hemophilia conference when a sudden pain shot through my head and face. It was more intense than any pain I had ever felt. Honestly, I thought I was having a brain aneurysm.

Thoughts flashed through my mind: what I had missed in life, what mattered, and what I still had left to do. I felt sad about all that I would miss out on. But, after five minutes had passed, I knew that it could not be an aneurysm; if it were, most likely, I would not have remained conscious, even if still alive. Nevertheless, it definitely was something serious. My face was swollen, and the tears just kept pouring out of my eyes. The man sitting next to me on the plane seemed very uncomfortable; he pretended not to notice, which was fine with me because I was uncomfortable as well, in addition to being in horrific pain.

I arrived in Montreal and went to the hotel, thinking that if I had a nap I might feel better. I tried to sleep but could not because the pain was too intense. I called the front desk to ask where I could find an English-speaking hospital, and then I called a cab and headed there. I was alone and did not know anyone attending this meeting; this was a new organization I had joined, and this was the first meeting. I was a little nervous that if something happened to me, no one would even notice. I felt that calling Curtis was not an option. The night before, while driving home, he had passed a man who'd been hit by a car and left dead on the side of the highway. As soon as he got home, Curtis called 911. The site of the accident was fairly close to our home, and we had seen the swarm of emergency workers heading to the scene, but we never heard anything else on it. Concerned that he needed more time to deal with that very recent situation, I did not want to call and worry him. Instead, I called my parents, gave them a short rundown of what was happening, and asked if they could just call the hospital every couple of hours to make sure everything was okay.

The ER took me in fairly quickly, because my face was so swollen. My eyes were almost swollen shut, but the tears continued pouring out of them. As you could imagine, I looked like a mess. After they had done X-rays and other tests, I waited to hear what this could be. Scared and alone, many different scenarios went through my mind during this time. Six very long hours later, the attending physician told me that he thought it was a severe case of facial neuralgia. He put me on antiseizure medication to help the nerves in my face settle, which would make the pain bearable. He advised me not to fly for a few days.

The next couple of days were crazy. I was on a lot of medication; plus, I was having trouble with balance, vision, and memory, and I wasn't sure whether these were side effects of the meds or caused by the neuralgia. Finally I was able to go home. The return flight to Toronto was delayed, which caused me to miss my connecting flight, necessitating an overnight stay in Toronto. I would be able to fly home the next morning, which, under ordinary circumstances, would not have been a very big deal, as Curtis would take care of the kids until I got home. But I could not remember much, and I could not walk right because my balance and vision both were impaired—so *everything* felt like a big deal. I was alone and very scared. Nevertheless, I made it home the next day, safe and sound— relatively speaking. My luggage was lost, but I did not care. I just wanted to be home.

I went to see a few more doctors to confirm the diagnosis. The pain was still extreme, and the side effects of the medications were awful; I was now taking prescription painkillers, to try to manage the relentless, intense pain. Months passed, but I did not improve. I struggled to take care of the kids, as I was in constant pain and still had problems with my balance and memory. None of the doctors I saw could offer me any other alternative treatments. Each day, I took my meds, but my body started rejecting them more and more. I became sicker and sicker. Barely able to get the meds down, I always felt completely unwell, in addition to the pain. The room never stopped spinning; and, even when I took the painkillers, my head constantly ached. Unable to concentrate or remember much, all I wanted to do was sleep.

Already feeling hopeless and frustrated with myself, I soon began to feel like I was dying inside. I had stopped taking the prescription painkillers because they made me feel even sicker, but one night I was in such severe pain that Curtis urged me to take them. I knew my husband was just trying to help, and I didn't really feel that I had any other options, so I took them. I fell asleep shortly thereafter, but I woke up a couple of hours later, with extreme pain in my stomach. Alarmed, Curtis called the ambulance. When I got to the hospital, they found that I had ulcers on the verge of bleeding. It felt like my body was shutting down. I kept telling Curtis how scared I was that I would not see the kids grow up. This was when I decided that what I was doing was not working, and I needed to find another way to deal with this condition.

From that moment, life started to turn around. As soon as I made the decision to start taking care of myself, everything changed—for the better. This was a struggle for me at first, because, at that point, I still believed that the more I gave, the better I was as a person. This is the "martyrdom belief system." By always putting myself last, I had now made myself so sick that I was not able to be a part of life. This was a huge struggle for my family. My husband worked out of town, with very long hours and minimal holidays. That meant that I had to be the main caregiver, and everything besides work outside the home fell on my shoulders. Of course, having a child with a serious health challenge made this an even greater responsibility. Everything seemed to be a constant struggle. It was like what would happen if the president of a company just did not show up for a year: things would just fall apart. It was a challenge, but I had faith that I could face it and overcome it. As always, I looked for what I was grateful for. For the first time in my whole life, I had seen the value of me. By becoming a parent, I automatically agreed to be the best I could be for my children's sake. My kids deserved my best, plain and simple. I remembered the promise I'd made to Braxton when I asked him to fight for his life, and now it was my turn. Again.

Utterly exhausted, I put up the white flag. I needed to find a doctor who would be able to help me take care of my son. I wanted to be a mom; I wanted to be part of life, to enjoy these moments with my kids. I did not want to fight for Braxton's healthcare anymore.

Months before, I had found a doctor in the next province, only a couple of hours away from where we lived. This doctor was willing to take Braxton as a patient. He had other hemophiliacs as patients, and he gave them excellent care. We met with him, and I felt such relief and happiness: I was not alone in all this any longer. Suddenly a knowing filled me, and I knew that he would help my son.

When I returned home after meeting with this doctor, I knew that we needed to move. Out of options, I was ready; Curtis was much more hesitant to move, but he did it anyway. Within two months we had moved, Curtis had transferred within his company, and this new part of our journey had started.

The kids and I loved our new home. Having the security of this doctor allowed me to start my own healing journey. The kids made new friends and started new activities. Life was smooth for us—finally. I should say that life was smooth for the kids and me. For Curtis, it was the opposite; he did not like his new job, which caused him to become very resentful and unhappy. This was hard, because Curtis was one of the happiest and most fun-loving people I have ever known. This had always been what I loved about him the most—and one of the reasons I held on through the toughest of times. When it came to Braxton's condition and the roughest of moments during our journey, Curtis always made us laugh. He would never give up being fun or seeing the kids smile. He would never let any of us stay down.

After a while of living in the new town and doing his new job, Curtis grew more and more unhappy. He came home one night and said that he could not do this job anymore. He went on to tell me that he had been offered a job back where we'd lived before. Curtis knew that, because of Braxton's challenges with healthcare, we would not be able to go with him. Curtis and I were both sad; I did not want him to be unhappy, but I was unwilling to put Braxton back in that danger. So he went back, and we stayed. We were still married, but as the months passed, Curtis detached more and more.

We both struggled with this difficult situation. Things continued to unravel, and our relationship became lost in a sea of untruths, insecurities, and resentment. Still unable to let go of our marriage but also unwilling to just "survive" in a marriage, we were unsure of our future together.

It was Easter, and we headed to the mountains to go on what I thought could be our last vacation together as a family. Every time we were in the mountains, Curtis dragged us out hiking, which was not my thing, but I went anyway. Halfway down the path, I begged Curtis to turn around; it was icy and dangerous. Curtis became very frustrated with this and was determined to keep going. Braxton was ahead of us, and, just as we got around the curve, he slipped on the ice, slid down the side of the mountain, and fell beneath the safeguard. Dangling over the edge of the mountain, Braxton hung on to the guard, looking at me with desperation to help him. He struggled to get up, fell a second time, and again was able to grab the railing.

Curtis took charge. Like a superhero, he leaped down the side of the mountain, grabbing Braxton and helping him up. Meanwhile, the crowd that had gathered just stood there in stunned silence. No one, least of all me, could believe what they had just seen.

Curtis and Braxton made it to safety. Blayne and I were in shock, and we could not stop crying. No one said a word as we turned back and headed to the car. All of our resentment—Curtis wanting to be in control of his own life, and my needing him to just be in my life—had come to head on this mountain, almost costing us a price that was far too high.

Just then Braxton turned to his dad, saying that his arm hurt from the jarring when he had grabbed the rail to keep from falling. At this point we were unsure if it was fractured or internally bleeding, so we started on the two-hour drive to the hospital. Braxton's arm was bleeding into the joint from the fall, but the alternative would have been falling off the mountain. We all felt grateful for the injury, as compared with what might have happened.

We put the kids to bed and then sat in the hall of the hotel. Feeling defeated and lost in this mess we had made of our marriage, I was tired of the fight, the untruths, the insecurities, and the resentment. I was now ready to let go of the marriage. What I craved the most was happiness, not only for me but for both of us. If we could not have happiness together, we were better off apart.

The wheels of fate once again started turning. Every Monday, I would scrapbook with a group of ladies. One particular Monday our little Chihuahua, Rockos, was sick, so I went home for lunch to check on him. He had gotten sick on his blanket, so I put it in the washer and then went back to scrapbooking. Most of the conversation that day was about how great everyone's husbands and marriages were. All I wanted to do was cry; my marriage was just about over, and I felt so alone. Saying I had a headache, I left scrapbooking early. When I got back to the house and opened my garage door, I saw water rushing from the house. Once inside, I found my dog swimming in a pool of water. There was so much water, the ceiling was caving in. A waterfall gushed right in the front doorway. My washer, which was upstairs, had malfunctioned; it kept running full force from the moment I had left two hours earlier until the moment I came home. All three levels of our home were damaged. I felt like my life and my house were in the same state at that moment: ruin. We found out that the whole house needed to be refinished, and we would be unable to live in it until the big renovations were complete. The kids and I had to live in the fifth-wheel trailer in the driveway, which meant Curtis did not have a place to stay, as he'd been living in the trailer. So he stayed with my parents, who lived in the same town where he worked.

Our life had crumbled, and we needed to rebuild it. With the kids and me needing the fifth-wheel trailer to live in, he had to stay with my parents until he could get the trailer back. Unable to sell the house, we decided that maybe we should use this time to see if we could work things out in our marriage. It had been over a year since Curtis had moved, and we had been living apart all that time. We did not know where, or how, to start. The journey of finding ourselves and what we wanted in our marriage, and our life, was at times very rocky. Knowing that nothing would change in our relationship if things stayed the same, we spent a lot of time rebuilding *us*. Sometimes we found it hard to say and hear each other's true feelings, and yet it seemed to be the only way to get through this challenge. For the first time in years, we were actually listening to each other instead of casting blame. With each issue we worked through, it became easier. This experience helped us develop new ways of communicating and better ways of treating each other. We did not erase old habits; we replaced them. In the end, we forged a deep friendship and found a mutual respect for each other, but neither one could have existed without this deep and often uncomfortable search. We now look forward to enjoying this life together instead of just surviving it.

Once Curtis and I worked things out, and started living joyfully again, things started to fall back into place. I found the combination of treatment that would help me control my facial neuralgia. While chatting with my hairdresser, I discussed the problem. She suggested seeing a naturopath doctor, which sounded like a good idea. It proved to be a great decision. I had my consultation with him, and he knew right away how he could help me. Within a week, I started feeling better. I continued seeing him for a year; things were going great, but I still was not 100 percent. He recommended an acupuncturist, and I committed to a year of treatment with her. At the end of that year, my whole body felt better. I literally felt my body coming back to life. We found that, by taking care of ourselves, our family became stronger. Part of living joyfully is having a balanced family, and achieving this balance starts with you! If you want to help others, you need to help yourself first.

GENTLE STEPS

Being the Authentic You

First, we need to figure out what's holding you back, and then we can plan the steps you need to take to fix it.

Are you living as the person you want to be?

Are you a player in your own life?

What can you do to align your life so that you put yourself back in your life?

Write down three things that you are committed to being (or becoming):

Who do you think you have to be?

Who do you have to be today in order to be more authentically *you* at the deepest level?

What are the action steps you can take, no matter how big or small, in order to become more authentically *you*?

Whatever those steps are, take them—or plan the steps to start taking them!

6

Blayne's Journey

Blayne has many special gifts: she lights up any room she is in, her hugs are like magic, and her spirit is wise! I asked her to write about her journey in her own words to help me understand her point of view. She shared the side of the younger sibling who often feels like a shadow (this can happen to older siblings too). Many times I was so exhausted from doing everything that I could in that moment, usually for Braxton's care, that I just didn't think about how much it all impacted Blayne. Discovering how left out she felt broke my heart. But I did not know what I could do better, or how I would find the energy to do it. I felt very frustrated that I was not doing well enough. I sought to find what was wrong in our relationship so that I could fix it, only to discover that what Blayne wanted the most was just to talk to me and my husband. She was not trying to hurt us; she just wanted to become a real part of the family where she often felt like she was no more than a shadow.

As much as it hurt to hear Blayne's authentic feelings, ignoring them will not make them go away. Ignoring feelings only feeds into fear, which does not deserve that power. One thing I explained to Blayne was that each person in the family sometimes needs to take the front seat, and the rest of the family needs to be there to uplift that person during the time of healing. This way, whether it was Braxton's time or Blayne's time or Curtis' time or my time, we were all there to understand the equal value of each individual. Talking with Blayne about her feelings is very important to her. Validating her feelings is one of the biggest keys to success that we have had. No judgment; just listening.

When Blayne's emotions become intense, she has asthma attacks, which frighten me significantly. One night I had a class, and Braxton was babysitting Blayne. They had a disagreement, and they both were very emotional charged. Blayne ended up having an asthma attack on the stairs. Curtis was out of town for work, and I missed the calls to my cell phone. By the time they got a hold of me, Blayne still was unable to catch her breath; the kids were alone, and Blayne just sat on the stairs, unable to breathe. When I got home I was frantic;

horrified thinking of what she had gone through, I was upset with the situation and wanted to find a way to empower Blayne to deal with her emotions.

My mission was to teach Blayne how to manage her emotions so that her emotions did not control her. I knew I didn't have the skills to teach her, so I began my search for someone, or something, that could. Tapping—or the Emotional Freedom Technique (EFT)—was something I discovered that I thought could work for her. She began using it, and she's had tremendous success. I formed many tapping programs in my business as a result of the success that Blayne has had.

Implementing this in our life did not happen overnight; rather, it was a process. We still work on her emotions each day. She loves to journal; actually, any creative outlet is like magic for Blayne. At night, I put on meditative music for her to help her relax and become balanced for the new day. I struggled with finding ways to make the time to do creative things with her, like coloring or scrapbooking, but I have found that the amount of time does not even matter. The most important thing for Blayne was, and still is, that I be one hundred percent engaged in the activity, and present in the moment, during "her time." No phone, no TV, no other people—just Blayne and me. This is something that still takes practice. There are those times when I feel so overwhelmed that I forget the importance of these things, but I just kept trying to be better at it. Blayne has always done this for our family; she always reminds us to slow down and enjoy the journey! Blayne is now ten years old, and I cannot imagine how much more she will teach us.

In Blayne's Own Words

My journey has been a bumpy road. My brother has hemophilia, so it's really bad when he gets hurt—and he always got hurt a lot. My brother knows his way around the Calgary Children's Hospital, the Medicine Hat Hospital, and many others. Well, I have asthma; it isn't as severe as hemophilia, but it is still really bad. So if I cannot stop crying, I know that I will have an asthma attack, and then I won't be able to breathe. I can have an asthma problem just from going by something I was allergic to, so I have to take asthma meds. It really sucks.

One thing I found to comfort me was my animals, and I have had many! Many of my animals have passed away, but I still love them. I have a kitten named Sugar and a dog named Rockos. I love them and feed them and play with them, but they are hard to keep up with. I still love them lots. All my animals make me happy.

My family loves to spend time together. Every summer we go camping, swimming, tubing, and boating. I have got to go to Disneyland and Disney World. It is fun just spending time together!

My brother, Braxton, got a wish from Children's Wish. I was happy that I did not have any bad illness, but I still felt sad that I did not get anything. But I was happy for my brother. Then he made my day when he shared his lion stuffy with a Children's Wish shirt with me.

Sometimes I feel like my brother gets more attention, especially when he gets hurt; my parents do not pay as much attention to me when I get hurt. That makes me feel mad, angry, and sad. It helps talking to my parents about my feelings, tapping (something my mom taught me how to do), giving my brother a hug, or cuddling with my kitten—that makes me feel happy and puts a smile on my face.

BLAYNE'S GENTLE STEPS

1. Your Feelings Matter

Talk with your family about your feelings. Don't keep your feelings hidden, and don't feel bad about them!

Come up with ways that you could spend time with your family:

Come up with ways to talk to your family about your feelings:

2. Journal

Start a journal where you write down your thoughts and feelings. This is a special journal, just for you!

3. Have Fun!

Spend time doing things that make you happy; for me, that is spending time with my animals or my friends, or working on crafts projects.

List what things you could do that would make you happy:

4. Relax

I listen to soothing music at bedtime; it makes me feel good and helps me sleep.

List things that would help you relax:

Braxton's Journey

Braxton's amazing spirit is so uplifting; combined with his sense of humor, he just shines. He always jokes, "Yep, I am the whole package!" Being true to yourself—and accepting who you are and all that you are—is true freedom, and that is one of Braxton's many gifts. Even when I would try to hold him back because of my own fears, he would never let my fears become his—and he would never let them hold him back. With his gentle, patient, and loving spirit, he would just wait for me to deal with my fears; as soon as I did, he would move on.

As a baby he was very patient and happy; he loved just *being*. He was not demanding or cranky, even when he was sick or injured; he just loved to be cuddled, and his world was good. As a toddler he loved to explore, and this caused some problems because of the constant risk of injury. I really struggled with his new adventurous side, trying my hardest to hold him back. I was so scared that he would get hurt; I just wanted to put him in a bubble of protection. Braxton, just wanting some freedom and independence, resisted this. Braxton started to act out, which I took very hard—and very personally. I cried so many tears with each new step of his independence. It took time, but we found our way. I gave him a little freedom, and he stopped acting out. This stage was hard for us, but we made it through, learning a lot of lessons in the process.

As patient as Braxton is, he does know what he wants and needs, and his trust in himself makes him very confident. As I've described, Braxton started administering his own IV meds when he was just nine years old! Many stood in amazement at his self-confidence. Meeting many children with chronic illnesses prior to this point, and knowing their strengths, we knew without a doubt that Braxton would succeed in self-care. However, it is an ongoing process. Now, when Braxton is hospitalized and someone comes into give him a needle or IV, he asks many questions about their plan for his care, and he will voice his opinion. If he feels that they are not picking the right vein, or that the needle is too big, he will tell them so. It is wonderful to watch this interaction, because most of the healthcare workers are awesome; they respect Braxton and his knowledge of his own body.

One time he was in the ER after transport by air ambulance for a broken arm. It had been a very turbulent flight, and so he was heavily medicated and hooked up to all sorts of monitors. He found that if he held his breath the monitor alarms would go off, and the nurse would come running back to check on him. In his medicated state—combined with the pain of his injury and the ever-present concern of internal bleeding, he found this extremely funny. He repeated the process of holding his breath about four times, until the nurse just stayed with him. The fun was over, but it was wonderful to see her kindness. Instead of becoming angry, she just stayed with him, and they started joking around. She understood that laughter was just what Braxton needed to get through this tough time, and so she gave it to him as part of his care.

Again, becoming a parent is not like anything you can imagine prior. I never knew what to expect once Braxton was born. Suffice it to say that, even though the journey was different than I had pictured, the results were far better—and more rewarding—than anything I ever could have imagined.

In Braxton's Own Words

My favorite memories of the times where I was hurt are of the time I spent in the Ronald McDonald House. That place was fun!

When I was in the hospital it seemed as though the Popsicles were endless, and that was always my mission: getting more Popsicles!

The one thing I struggled with the most was not being able to play ice hockey. Hockey is my favorite sport, and I wanted to play so bad. After years of trying to convince my parents to let me play ice hockey, we compromised with ball hockey. It's a noncontact sport, so my parents thought I could give it a try. That was a few years ago, and I am still playing my favorite position: goalie. My second-favorite sport is basketball. I enjoy watching all sports, and I spend a lot of time catching up with my sports shows in the morning, afternoon, and evening.

Most of all, I just enjoy being me!

BRAXTON'S GENTLE STEPS

Be True to Yourself

Being true to yourself—and accepting who you are and all you are—is true freedom!

What are some things you already accept about yourself?

What are some things you still need to learn to accept about yourself?

What are your favorite things about yourself?

Accept and enjoy the power of being *you!*

Final Thoughts

I have no doubt that the human spirit's amazing strength and passion can conquer all fears and transform all negativity to positivity. Some people wander through life, allowing circumstances and other individuals to shape their identity. Once you recognize and appreciate all the great gifts you possess, you will be able to shape your life. This is true for each and every one of us.

It is not the moments in life that make you; it is what you do in those moments. Once you believe that you have the key to improving your life, you can—and will—do it. It takes more than just wishing that you had the key; you can't be ready to do something until you believe that you can do it. When your journey in life is not what you planned, be open to letting the light shine in anyway—it just may surprise you! Life is an adventure; we are here to discover, grow, play, and learn. At one point or another, we each face difficult situations. Remember to see problems as opportunities and obstacles as challenges. Believe in yourself, and appreciate the gift of your life.

When facing a difficult situation:

- First, take a minute to breathe.
- Next, decide what you are going to make of the situation.
- Remind yourself that you, and only you, control your reactions; only you can decide how each situation will play a part in your life.
- Trust yourself to make the right decision.

We all have the same ability to take the steps I have described in this book. This ability is not just for a lucky few; it is for everyone. We each just have to uncover it. Through the gentle steps in this book, you will start dusting off the precious jewel and light that lives in you! You can only advance by being larger than your present place.

I am so grateful that you have taken this journey with me; I hope my words serve you well.

WORKBOOK

Gentle Steps for Healing your heart

GENTLE STEPS: THE DIAGNOSIS

I know that nearly everyone has heard of how therapeutic journaling is, and I am going to say it again.

1. Start to Journal

I started one a **journal** and divided it into **four sections:**

- **Section 1** is where I journal my own thoughts.
- **Section 2** is where I journal my thoughts for my son.
- **Section 3** is where I journal my thoughts for my daughter (you will meet her a bit later on in the book).
- **Section 4** is where I journal my thoughts for my husband.

I also started a **gratitude journal.** Every day, I write about one thing that I am thankful for. This ensures that I always feel grateful, and that alone has gotten me far!

Never underestimate the attitude of gratitude!

No one saw my journals; as a result, journaling allowed me to release and share my thoughts when I was unable to voice them. It still does.

I was frightened of the whole idea of journaling. I was taught to keep my feelings inside, so I never knew how to express my feeling. Bringing light to those feelings can be very frightening at first. However, whether or not you admit your feelings, they are there, and bottling them up can do a lot more damage than releasing them. When you are aware of your feelings you are able to validate them, which is incredibly freeing.

Below are some examples to help you start your own journal. Once you begin to journal, just continue to write whatever thoughts and feelings come to your mind. It doesn't have to be organized—or even make sense—just continue to write and release your emotions. Remember, this is your journal, and there is no right or wrong way to journal!

2. Examples of How to Start

- I am so frustrated that the doctor . . . *sometimes does not listen.*
- I am so frustrated that my friend . . . *does not understand what I am going through.*
- I feel like I missed out on . . . *moments being the way I thought they would be.*
- These are the words that describe my life . . . *remarkable and blessed or chaotic and exhausting*
- I am so grateful for . . . *getting a peaceful shower today so I had a couple minutes to myself.*
- I love it when . . . *I get a surprise.*
- I am so grateful that my husband . . . *had the coffee ready for me when I got up.*
- I am so grateful that my child . . . *gave me a hug this morning. That set me up for a great day!*

Now write some of your own:

3. Have a Positive Conclusion

Always end your journaling on a positive note; conclude with your grateful thoughts, so you are in the attitude of gratitude. (It's up to you if you want to start a separate gratitude journal as well.) Make sure you keep it simple. Don't overthink it—you don't want journaling to become another "job" or item on your to-do list. Journaling should be something that helps you, and also that you have fun with. Make it your own process; there is no right or wrong method. Every moment, no matter how big or small, is a piece of your life's puzzle, so enjoy the journey of your life!

GENTLE STEPS: THE TRIALS

1. Evaluate Your Belief System

Ask yourself, *What is my belief system?*

Your belief system is made from beliefs you have been taught about situations in life—about money, work, or anything. Often we adapt these beliefs to our lives, never challenging them to see if they still serve us in the present moment. As we change and grow, so do our needs—and so can our beliefs. We must have an open awareness of why we do what we do, as this is the only honest way to see if it still works for us. Being aware of your belief system—and being open to letting go of those beliefs that no longer serve you—will help you grow in all areas of your life. Your belief system can limit you, unconsciously, from achieving your goals. In answering the next questions be very honest and take your time.

What are the limitations that keep you from achieving your goals?

What are your beliefs around those limitations?

Do you feel that your beliefs still serve you, or are you open to challenging them?

What new beliefs would work to replace limitations in your situation?

What are the pros and cons of the new belief(s)?

What limitations do you put on your loved ones?

What are your beliefs around those limitations?

Do you feel that your beliefs still serve you, or are you open to challenging them?

What new beliefs would work to replace the limitations in your situation?

What are the pros and cons of the new beliefs?

2. Never Underestimate the Value of You!

This section is dedicated to giving you the credit you deserve. Often we do not give ourselves credit for our accomplishments, big or small, and this kind of credit is very important. As you accomplish things in your life, use them as stepping-stones to build you up. This may be hard, but it is so important; think back on all the things that you're proud of, and write them down. Acknowledge *you*.

List the top five accomplishments of each one of your family members, big and small, that make you proud. You could have each one of your family members do this, and then share with each other. This would help everyone establish an attitude of gratitude!

1.

2.

3.

4.

5.

3. Contact Support

Support groups can be found through the hospital, Internet, or phone book.

It can be so helpful to have someone to talk to. Perhaps you have a good friend or family member to share with. Often it can also be helpful to have others who have been in the same situation. There are many ways you can find support, depending on what you are going through. Finding others who know how you feel can make you feel less isolated; they also can guide you, based on their own experience.

GENTLE STEPS: LIVING LIFE

In order to be fulfilled you need to grow and contribute!

1. Design Your Ideal Day

From the moment you wake up until you go to bed, plan your ideal day:

These are the things that you can try to start putting into your day until this becomes a natural part of how you live every day. If you want to live more joyfully, you have to start adding things to your everyday routine that make you more joyful. Even the small things make a big difference. Now I know you may already be starting a list of reasons why you cannot do this, so here is step 2.

2. See Limits as Opportunities!

Turn all your "I can't _____" statements into "I am open to _____" statements:

As long as you make yourself believe that you can't, you will never be open to change. Once you are open to change, you will be amazed at what can happen. By being open to seeing in other ways, you will be able to see a bigger view, and realize that you have more options. By eliminating the word *can't* from your vocabulary, the excuses go away, and you realize all that is left is opportunity!

3. Control Your Fears and Design Your Dreams!

If you feel fear about something, somewhere in your life you are not prepared for this next step. Find the area where you need to strengthen, and then the fear will no longer exist.

Here is an example. If you are scared of water, you can do one of two things: never go near water again, or realize that this is an area that needs to be strengthened. If you choose the latter you could go get proper swimming lessons, which would strengthen the area where you feel fear. As you prepare yourself your fear will lessen, and you will eventually be able to swim. Also realize that fear is a warning and a gift: it lets you know that you have a weak area, and you need to prepare to handle the situation. By being aware of the fears and areas that need to be strengthened, you will be able to control the fear and design your dreams!

What are your fears?

Which areas does your fear make you aware that you need to strengthen?

What action steps can you take to strengthen those areas?

GENTLE STEPS: LETTING GO

1. Learning to Let Go

Below are the questions I described asking myself at the beginning of this chapter. Now it's your turn to ask and answer them, in terms of your and your family's experiences.

Where can I improve in order to help my kids and myself?

How well have I prepared them and myself for this next step?

What can I do to prepare them and myself in a healthy and nonintrusive manner?

What actions do I need to take in order to help them and myself?

2. Live the Life You Choose!

Now you need to determine whether the way you are living your life is the way that you *choose* to live your life.

Ask yourself, "Why am I doing what I am doing in my life?"

Now ask yourself, "Does what I do align me with my highest values and fondest dreams?"

If your fearful motivations drive your answers to the above, you can do one of two things: change *what* you are doing with your life, or change *why* you are doing it.

3. The "Inspired Why"

The truth is, you may not be able to change the *what,* but you probably can change the *why*—or at least your approach to it. If changing the *what* is not an option, create an **"inspired why"**! That is, redefine the *why* of where you are now until you can change the situation (i.e., the *what*). This *why* will help you live life as you choose; it will help you create a life filled with joy. That's what an **inspired why** is! If you understand and are deeply inspired by this *why,* eventually, you will begin to connect with others whom your *why* will also inspire; they will want to support and encourage you, and that will help you carry your *why*. Your *why* should be powered by your heart, not your head. Become crystal clear about your *why;* love it and live it!

Create *your* "inspired why":

4. Live Life with Purpose!

This goes back to what I said earlier about finding something bigger than the hurt and the fear, as this will help you let go of that fear and pain. First, make a **"purpose statement."** The real purpose of life is life itself! You need to live this life, enjoy this life, and embrace this life by living in the uniqueness of you! Here is a purpose statement that might help you create your own:

> *The purpose of my life is to be fully <u>alive</u> and <u>vibrant</u>, to enjoy this life living in the uniqueness of me, to adore and appreciate my loved ones, to guide others to feel fully alive, and to strengthen and share my gifts so that I might inspire others to strengthen and share their own gifts.*

Create *your* purpose statement, underlining the words that are most important to you, as in the example above:

Now, using the words that are most meaningful to you (i.e., the ones you underlined), answer the questions that follow. [Below, I have used the words that I underlined as examples; please use your own words in order to derive the most meaning from this exercise.]

What make you feel more alive and vibrant?

Whatever that is, do more of it!

What are you gifts?

Whatever they are, share them more often!

The above exercises have helped you make a "map" of what makes you feel positive and happy. Incorporating more of those things in your life will allow you to experience more positive emotion!

GENTLE STEPS: OUR JOURNEY AS PARENTS

Being the Authentic You

First, we need to figure out what's holding you back, and then we can plan the steps you need to take to fix it.

Are you living as the person you want to be?

Are you a player in your own life?

What can you do to align your life so that you put yourself back in your life?

Write down three things that you are committed to being (or becoming):

Who do you think you have to be?

Who do you have to be today in order to be more authentically *you* at the deepest level?

What are the action steps you can take, no matter how big or small, in order to become more authentically *you*?

Whatever those steps are, take them—or plan the steps to start taking them!

GENTLE STEPS: BLAYNE'S JOURNEY

1. Your Feelings Matter

Talk with your family about your feelings. Don't keep your feelings hidden, and don't feel bad about them!

Come up with ways that you could spend time with your family:

Come up with ways to talk to your family about your feelings:

2. Journal

Start a journal where you write down your thoughts and feelings. This is a special journal, just for you!

3. Have Fun!

Spend time doing things that make you happy; for me, that is spending time with my animals or my friends, or working on crafts projects.

List what things you could do that would make you happy:

4. Relax

I listen to soothing music at bedtime; it makes me feel good and helps me sleep.

List things that would help you relax:

GENTLE STEPS: BRAXTON'S JOURNEY

Be True to Yourself

Being true to yourself—and accepting who you are and all you are—is true freedom!

What are some things you already accept about yourself?

What are some things you still need to learn to accept about yourself?

What are your favorite things about yourself?

Accept and enjoy the power of being you!

GENTLE STEPS: FINAL THOUGHTS

When facing a difficult situation:

- First, take a minute to breathe.
- Next, decide what you are going to make of the situation.
- Remind yourself that you, and only you, control your reactions; only you can decide how each situation will play a part in your life.
- Trust yourself to make the right decision.

We all have the same ability to take the steps I have described in this book. This ability is not just for a lucky few; it is for everyone. We each just have to uncover it. Through the gentle steps in this book, you will start dusting off the precious jewel and light that lives in you! You can only advance by being larger than your present place.

To learn more about Clara Penner and her programs, please visit:

EFT Personal Developments Inc.

www.eftpersonaldevelopments.ca

If you like this program, you may also like:

- Gentle Steps on the Journey of the Healing Heart for a Caregiver
- Gentle Steps on the Journey of the Healing Heart for Yourself
- Gentle Steps on the Journey of the Healing Heart for Parents

These programs guide you in dealing with the intense emotions that accompany these difficult times. The goal is to walk with you as you find yourself again, helping you achieve balance and providing you with tools for dealing with the intense emotions. Healing begins by taking care of *you,* so you are able to give care to your loved ones and build strong, healthy relationships. All three programs are offered as live events or online where we go through the program together, step by step. You can join in the comfort of your own home, or live, whichever works for you. To find out more about these programs, please visit:

www.eftpersonaldevelopments.ca.

Or send an e-mail to:

eftpersonaldevelopments@hotmail.com.

Wishing you the best of everything!